Foreword

This booklet, the second in a series of training manuals, is intended as an introduction to post production work in film and videotape particularly for those new to programme making. These days it is no longer quite as common as it used to be for aspiring film or television makers to work in cutting rooms, studios or other technical areas before venturing into programme production work. A good grounding in the complexities and technical processes of film or videotape has always been regarded as a useful (some would say essential) pre-requisite for a young director, but today relatively few newcomers to television production have had such a practical apprenticeship. Production staff new to television often find themselves in cutting rooms or editing suites armed with only the most rudimentary knowledge of the stages necessary to turn their tapes or film rushes into a finished product. Their knowledge of professional and technical terminology is also, inevitably, limited. It is true that this lack of knowledge is generally quickly recognised — and with the help of sympathetic editors, rectified — but ignorance of the working procedures in a cutting room or editing suite can be a frustrating, not to say embarrassing, experience.

The purpose of this manual is to provide an outline of the principal steps involved in film and videotape editing along with a number of hints and suggestions aimed at helping the inexperienced programme maker towards a confident approach to post production techniques. *Editing Film and Videotape* is not intended to be definitive or comprehensive, but contains the kind of information that is basic to an understanding of film and videotape editing. It has been written in the conviction that while good film and television programmes are always planned, produced and directed *outside* the cutting room or editing suite, what goes on inside is of vital importance to the quality and creativity of the final product.

Gordon Croton

Head of BBC Television Training

EDITING FILM AND VIDEOTAPE

Ed Boyce

Mike Crisp

Peter Jarvis

BBC *Television Training Manuals*

Already published:
SHOOTING ON LOCATION
EDITING FILM AND VIDEOTAPE
FROM SCRIPT TO SCREEN: DOCUMENTAR
STAND BY STUDIO!
AFTER TEA WE'LL DO THE FIGHT:
    FILMING ACTION
DIRECTING SITUATION COMEDY
CONTINUITY NOTES

First published in 1986 by
BBC Television.Training
BBC Elstree Centre
Clarendon Road
Borehamwood
Hertfordshire

Revised Edition 1989

© 1986 BBC Television Training
All rights reserved
ISBN 0 948694 05 X

General Editor: Gordon Croton

Design and production: Shirley Greenfield

Graphics: Peter Kendall

Photographs: Mike Cullen

Printed by BBC Print Unit, Evesham,
England

Film Editing

When a Director has finished shooting a film or videotape on location, he or she is still only half-way to a final product fit for showing. The processes which ensue are known collectively as Post Production. Although there are only minor differences between the techniques of shooting film or videotape, the differences at the post production stage are quite marked.

Most film for professional use is shot on a **Separate Magnetic (Sepmag)** system. This means that the sound is recorded separately but synchronously on a quarter-inch tape recorder at the time of filming. In professional television production, sound and pictures thereafter remain apart throughout all stages up to transmission.

There is an alternative system called **Combined Magnetic (Commag)** in which there is a recording mechanism in the camera and the film carries a magnetic stripe along its edge. As the point at which the sync sound is recorded is several frames removed from the relevant frame of picture, it is impossible to make simultaneously a clean sound and picture cut. Commag was once popular for News filming but has now been almost wholly replaced by video. It survives, however, as a format for the amateur Super 8 film-maker.

THE STAGES: RUSHES TO SHOW PRINT

At the end of a shoot, the Cameraman is responsible for sending his exposed film rushes to the laboratories with instructions about processing. The Sound Recordist delivers his spools of sound to a **Sound Transfer Suite** where the quarter-inch tapes are transferred on to sprocketed 16mm magnetic tape. Both transferred sound and processed film are returned to the **Film Cutting Room**. From now on, unless major problems arise calling for a re-shoot, the job of the film crew is finished.

The key person alongside the Director now is the Film Editor. On very large productions, there may be several cutting rooms operating in tandem under a Supervising Editor. There may also be separate Picture and Sound Editors. But in most television productions, it is normal to employ a single Editor helped by an Assistant Editor.

The film editing process consists of a series of distinct operations; syncing up, logging, rubber numbering, breaking down, assembling, negative cutting, track-laying and dubbing. Although the processes follow a single logical sequence, there is hardly a stage before the final mix of the dub when changes cannot be carried out. This flexibility results from being able to re-cut and join film at any point in a programme without having to make changes elsewhere and also from the fact that all sound is manipulated separately from the picture. This infinite flexibility means that the Director can edit and re-edit any number of times to the accuracy of a single frame. This is one reason for the continuing popularity of film as a production medium. Current systems of videotape editing still lack this post production flexibility.

Film Editing

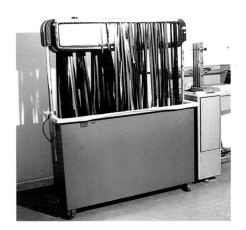

Cutting room: trim bin

*Examples of key numbers (left);
rubber numbers (right)*

The first step in the film editing process is when the Assistant Editor syncs up the rushes. When the sound is recorded on location the camera and recorder will not have been switched on at identical times and the machines themselves have different 'run up' times. Camera and recorder hold sync only for the duration of a take. A clear indicaton of sync is therefore needed for every shot. The **clapperboard** provides this. Syncing up involves identifying each take from the information on the clapperboards, finding the frame on the film where the clapper hits the board and then listening to the sound track to hear the verbal identification of the shot and the sound of the 'clap'. By marrying up sound and picture from the clapperboard on each successive take, the Assistant builds up rolls of synchronised rushes. The Editor and the Director are now in a position to view the film.

At this stage the Editor will have to decide whether **rubber numbering** is necessary. This is a simple aid to the identification of sounds and pictures in the cutting rooms and involves mechanically printing a sequence of matching numbers along the edges of the picture and sound. These rubber numbers should not be confused with the so-called **key numbers** which are printed along the edge of the negative by the manufacturer. They are important to the negative cutter who uses them as a reference for matching the frames of film in the finished cutting copy with the frames of the original negative.

In short, **key numbers** provide a reference between cutting copy picture and its appropriate negative. They are printed into the negative at the time of manufacture and transferred photographically to the rush prints as part of the usual printing process. **Rubber numbers** provide a sync reference between cutting copy picture and cutting copy sound. They are printed on to the picture and sound rolls after the syncing up process.

One more important routine takes place before the creative process of editing can start. The Assistant Editor notes the front and end key number and the front and end rubber number of each slate (clapperboard number). This is known as **logging the rushes**.

The process takes time but is a vital aid in locating the shots during the later stages of the editing process. If rushes have been properly logged, a single key number or rubber number reference can identify the slate number, take number and also reveal how much more of the shot exists.

As the Assistant Editor logs the rushes he or she also breaks down the rushes rolls into their individual slates. The Editor can now select sound and picture of any shot on demand — the parts of the shot which are not selected for inclusion in the rough cut are labelled and hung on individual pegs in the **trim bin** so they are immediately available for any alterations. Again, the logging process can be a boon in identifying which trim goes with which slate.

The Director or his Production Assistant will have provided the Editor with a detailed **shot list** (see p.8), which has been kept during the shooting. This contains the number of each slate together with a detailed description of the shot and its duration.

From the shot list, the Director should usually have worked out a rough **assembly order** or **assembly script** (see p.9), which gives the Film Editor an idea of the intended shape of the programme. Even in drama productions where a script is available, an assembly order is essential because scenes are rarely shot in sequence and a great deal of time can be saved if good and bad takes are identified on paper in the first place.

At this stage, the Director can probably leave the Editor alone to make up the first **assembly** or **rough cut**. Whilst this is going on, the Director can go away to arrange any music, rostrum camera work, or additional library film that has so far been put off or overlooked. However, it is obviously important — not least for the time-scale of the production — that as much material as possible should be made ready in advance.

Although Directors are often tempted to spend most of their time in the cutting room it is probably good practice on most productions to leave the Editor to work on the assembly in his own way and to arrive at a style and tempo of cutting that will provide the basis for later discussions in the cutting room. Certainly most Film Editors seem to prefer this way of working.

Depending on the type of production (drama, documentary, current affairs, dance, etc.) and the amount of time available, the **assembly** can vary from a rough blocking-out of themes and sequences to a complex, thought-through guide (see p.9). A News Film Editor, for example, would expect to be given a very detailed cutting order and even a written script to work from and be ready with a near-finished product with only minutes to spare for final alterations.

When the Director returns to view the **rough cut**, alterations may suggest themselves. In the case of a complex documentary shot over many months, there may be any number of revisions, re-assemblies and re-cuts. The only final determinants are the

contd. p.11

Motorised pic sync

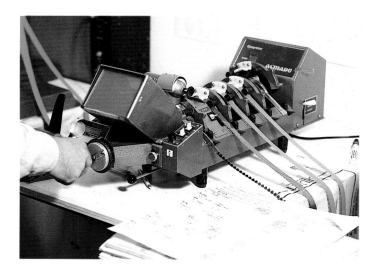

Specimen: Shot List

<table>
<tr><td>Strand/Series Title</td><td colspan="5"></td><td colspan="3">**SHOOTING ORDER SHOT LIST**</td></tr>
<tr><td>Programme Title</td><td colspan="5"></td><td colspan="2">Distribution</td><td colspan="2">Denotes Recipient ↘</td><td>No of Cop</td></tr>
<tr><td>Episode/ Sub. Title</td><td colspan="5"></td><td colspan="2">To:-</td><td colspan="2">Room No. and Building</td><td>✓</td></tr>
<tr><td rowspan="2">Costing Number</td><td rowspan="2" colspan="3"></td><td>Prod. Costing Wk(s)</td><td>Channel</td><td colspan="3">Film Editor:</td><td>*</td><td>1</td></tr>
<tr><td rowspan="2"></td><td rowspan="2"></td><td rowspan="2" colspan="3">Snr. Asst. Enquiries Film Library</td><td rowspan="2"></td><td rowspan="2">1</td></tr>
<tr><td>Programme Identificat'n Number</td><td colspan="3"></td><td>Studio</td></tr>
<tr><td>Production date(s)</td><td colspan="3"></td><td>Week(s)</td><td></td><td colspan="4"></td></tr>
<tr><td>Filming/O.B. date(s)</td><td colspan="3"></td><td>Week(s)</td><td></td><td colspan="4"></td></tr>
<tr><td></td><td colspan="3"></td><td colspan="2">Room No. / Building</td><td>Tel. Extn.</td><td>Department</td><td colspan="2">File Copy | 1</td></tr>
<tr><td>Producer Director Designer</td><td colspan="3"></td><td colspan="3"></td><td colspan="3">Date *</td></tr>
</table>

To assist Film Library, please give full details of Location for each camera roll No.

Camera Roll No.	Slate No.	Take	Description	Sound	Tape No.	Duration
			Sierra Leone 12 June (contd.)			
			Exteriors, Freetown			
62	465	I BoE	WS Freetown from Parliament Building – from town pan R to sea	S	33	40"
	466	I	As 465 but pan L from sea to town (? dissolve from rostrum shot map to this)	S		
	467	I BoE	From sea pull out to include town (NG)	M		25"
	467	2	A/B (OK)	M		
	468	I	Pan L from sea as pull out slowly to inc. town	M		
			From Lestor Peak road – clouds coming down			
	469	I	HA Freetown with trees f/g in silhouette	M		25"
	470	I BoE	Similar from slightly different angle	M		
	471	I BoE	Similar but slightly wider	M		
			Atmos. to cover 469 – 471	W/T		
			Number One Beach			
	472	I BoE	Pan L off sea to along beach, and back R to sea	S		30"
	473	I BoE	More, similar	S		
	474	I	Shooting along beach in opposite direction with land R (some Europeans on beach)	S		
	475	I	More, similar, posed. Further R	S		
			13 June			
			Freetown Cheshire Home			
			Girls breakfasting on balcony			
			Heavy rain	W/T		
	476	I	From WS boys' house pan L to LS balcony as Home Mother in to serve b.fast to waiting girls (cam. not happy)	S		15"
	477	I BoE	From boys' house pan L to LS balcony and girls waiting with food in front of them - slow zoom to group	S		30"

Abbreviations A/B — as before atmos — atmosphere BoE — board on end f/g — foreground LS — long shot
M — mute M & E — music and effects NG — no good S — sync sound WS — wide shot W/T — wild track

Specimen: Assembly Order

A WORLD OF DIFFERENCE

Assembly Order (contd.)

Picture	Outline (Commentary)
Philip Mason 31/1 from – 'Things I can't do – (to) – because they can't speak' (possibly cutaway on 'activities' to 36/2 or 3)	
Irish street scenes with collections etc. Best from 237/1 – 253/2 (also see below)	But this is not so much a film about particular handicaps or individuals. It's about what has been called the fragility of human compassion – the problems posed by our own embarrassment, guilt and fear in the face of disability ... Thousands of television viewers who would normally at least <u>start</u> to watch a documentary programme won't have switched on this film – because of its subject ... There's no doubt that there is an abysmal <u>lack</u> of accurate information about disability just as there's an appalling <u>wealth</u> of misinformation, prejudice and superstition ... (talking heads)
Ken Roberts 616/1 from – 'I remember once being in a pub – (to) – in the box on the bar or something like that'	
Snowy Harding 13/1 from – 'I don't think I've taken – (to) – let them get on with it'	
Liz Briggs 22/1 from – 'I think people ought to realise – (to) – and thumping him one'	
Irish street scenes Best from 237 – 253/2 NB collecting tin shot 239/1 (? use pan from crowd)	Somehow this street scene – familiar enough in many Western cities – filmed in Dublin last year – underlines our dilemma. In 1980 there were X number (figure to come) of street collections in Dublin alone for charity, most of them for organisations working on behalf of the handicapped. For many of us a few pence placed from time to time in a collecting tin in the street or on a pub bar represents our only investment in or recognition of physical handicap ...
2. Historical Section	Music – Schubert's Trio No.1 Op.99 2nd Movement Yet, perhaps it's not surprising, because from the earliest times disability has been viewed in Western society with at best embarrassment and at worst horror and shame.
Details of bench shooting and dupe film to be provided separately NB Commentary written to specific stills, etc.	Disabled people have so often been treated as extra-social beings and ostracised and degraded. For centuries disability, like poverty, was regarded as just punishment for sin. In the 17th century religious leaders like Martin Luther and John Calvin both expressed the belief that mentally handicapped people were filled with Satan. In Britain in the 19th century the Eugenics Movement was founded by Sir Francis Galton. It was a movement which

Specimen: Cue Sheet

SYNC MARKS EVERY 50' 35MM FEET

PRODUCTION: THE RETURN OF TRUSCOTT REEVE JOB NO. I/ATT F433N REEL NO. I OF 2 PAGE 5

PRODUCER/DIRECTOR: MIKE CRISP EDITOR: CHRISTINE BOOTH

ACTION	1	2	3 FILTER	4	5 FILTER	6 NO FILTER	7 DISK MUSIC
TOM ON STUDIO FLOOR			..trying to think" 210			↓ STUDIO ATMOS	
212½					212½		
W/S GALLERY 215	214 FRANK "Ha!"				STUDIO ATMOS	212½	
217							
C/U FRANK GALLERY	218 "That last clip...						
221½	... pretty amazing"	221½			FILTER		
MARCUS GALLERY	221½	MARCUS 222 "Yes, I thought..			↓		
	225	...like it" 224					
	FRANK 226 "What's it from" 227	225½	226 TOM 228 "It's from		STUDIO ATMOS		
	228		...years" 230				
231		231					
FRANK GALLERY		FRANK "Who directed Tom?"	232				
234	234					234	
TOM + GARY ON STUDIO FLOOR	TOM "Not sure...!	234			234	STUDIO ATMOS NO FILTER	
242½	...you're right" 242½	242½			242½	242½	
STELLA + MARCUS GALLERY	+ ATMOS ↓	STELLA "Clever old Gary" ↓			STUDIO ATMOS FILTER		

10

Dubbing theatre: Sepmag bay

Dubbing theatre: control desk

subject matter, time and money. Clearly, the more the Director has worked out his aims and achieved his ends during the shooting, the less time is spent fruitlessly re-jigging the rushes.

When the sequence of shots has been agreed, there only remains the **fine cut** stage in which the Editor works to improve the slickness of the finished film by trimming or adding various frames or making fine adjustments to the sync track.

If the fine cut meets with the approval of all concerned, there follows the process of **track-laying**. During the editing process, the Editor cuts the sound to match the picture on one or two reels, but, when he and the Director have finalised the picture editing, the sound is 'track-laid' on the synchroniser. First of all the sync tracks — that is the sound that was shot at the same time as the picture — are split. For Shot 1 the sync sound is on Track 1 and there is blank spacing on Track 2. The picture and tracks are wound down to the first change of shot and here the first split takes place. The sound for Shot 2 is joined on to Track 2, which was previously blank spacing, and the blank spacing is transferred to Track 1. The footage where this occurs is noted on a **cue sheet** (see p.10). This is a pictorial representation of the tracks which will be of vital assistance to the dubbing mixer later on. This process continues right through to the end of the film until the sound is in two reels with alternate spacing and sound on each. With the sound on two tracks, the dubbing mixer can set his mixer controls at two separate levels and thus, any differences in recording level on the track, can be 'ironed out'.. A further technique of track splitting is that wherever possible the Sound Editor will provide an overlap at the front and end of each track split. The front and end trim of each sound take is added to the appropriate track. (**Rubber numbers** are particularly useful for this process). Now there is sound available before and after each picture cut. A sound mix is a much smoother transition for the ear to accept. When the tedious process of track splitting is over, the more creative part of the process takes place. Wild tracks shot on location as 'atmosphere fillers' are laid-up on Track 3, spot effects on Track 4 and music on Track 5, etc. The whole of this is pictorially represented on the cue sheets, often called dubbing charts (see *Specimen* on p.10).

Track-laying is a time-consuming process and it should always be allowed for in the editing schedule. Do not plan to finish fine cutting a 50-minute documentary on Monday when the dub is on Wednesday. An average 50-minute film will need 5 days track-laying and track-laying cannot begin until the picture has been fine cut.

The finalised cutting copy, together with the tracks, is taken to a **Dubbing Theatre**. The sound tracks are each placed on a player synchronously locked to a projector. The Dubbing Mixer mixes the various tracks to order in relation to the projected film, whilst his Assistant may play in extra effects from an

Film Editing

effects disc or quarter-inch tape. It is possible to spin-in spot effects, such as car door slams and gun shots, but it is far wiser to confine the disc facilities in the dubbing theatre to the playing-in of general background effects (sea wash, traffic, birds singing, etc.) As a rule of thumb, spot effects and music should always be laid by the Sound Editor. In the same way, it is also preferable if other general effects are laid as well, but you can spin them in at the dub if the track-laying time is at a premium. It is usual to mix all Music and Effects down on to a single track, generally referred to as the **M. & E. mix**. It may also be necessary to record a **commentary** track, in which case the programme Presenter will come to the dubbing theatre. Modern dubbing theatres are highly sophisticated and it is possible to stop, start and re-play any track and re-dub any sequence without having to go back to the top of the film. This is known as **rock-and-roll dubbing**. When the M. & E. track and the commentary are regarded as complete, the dubbing mixer does a **final mix** to combine and balance the two. Remember that once music and effects have been combined on the M. & E., the relative levels of effects and music are fixed and cannot be adjusted when the commentary is added, i.e. reducing the level of the M. & E. track under the commentary will reduce both effects and music. This sometimes leads to problems and, in difficult cases, it may be wiser to do an effects pre-mix and then add commentary and music together, thus having independent control over the levels of effects, music and commentary (or dialogue). In such a case, the M. & E, which is vital for foreign language versions, can be made *after* the final mix. The film sound process is now complete.

It is common, when time allows, to dub the film using what is known as a **slash dupe**. This is a film print taken directly from the cutting copy with no attempt to grade shots. Its use has certain advantages because an edited film can contain so many tape joins that it could become untrustworthy in the dubbing theatre projector. Also while track-laying and dubbing are being done on the slash dupe, the original cut film can be sent off for negative cutting.

Negative cutting

Negative cutting can either be done at the laboratories or by one of a number of specialist firms. Using a synchroniser similar to that used in the cutting room, the negative cutter takes the original film negative and cuts this to match up exactly with the cutting copy. This is achieved by using the key numbers on the cutting copy and negative as a reference.

The negative is cut and joined with film cement to provide an exact negative for the finished programme. When film is cement-joined there is a slight overlap of film at each join. Unlike 35mm film, 16mm has a very thin frame line between each frame, therefore, if the negative is cut as a single reel, the cement overlap can show up as an aggravating white line flash on each negative join. In order to make the negative joins invisible, 16mm film is **chequerboard neg. cut** — that is, the negative is cut on two synchronous rolls with alternate negative and spacing on each roll. The negative joiners are designed so that the cement joins overlap into the spacing area and never appear when the two negative rolls are combined for the final print. Chequerboard negative cutting, sometimes inaccurately called **A&B negative cutting**, has another great advantage. If the negative on roll A continues *beyond* the point of a cut and the negative on roll B starts *before* the point of a cut, the printer can be cued to fade from one negative to the other and thus create a picture mix. It should be added that A&B mixes are the only optical effects that can be achieved in the standard printing process and that they work best when mixing scenes of similar density.

Colour grading

When the **printing stage** is reached the cut negative is passed to a technician known as a Colour Grader who decides if the variation in exposure contrast and colour balance in successive shots needs any correction. He prepares a programme on punch tape which will instruct the printing machine to make the necessary corrections when the cut negative is printed. This cue tape also contains the information as to where A&B mixes occur. The film is then printed and the print is returned to the cutting room.

Prints

The first print is known as the first **answer print**, and if all is well, may be good enough for transmission. But if the Director requires further adjustments to colours, etc., the laboratory will be contacted and further answer prints may be requested until everyone is satisfied. The final print is the **show print** and together with the **final mix** of the dubbed sound, is the completed programme.

With films scheduled for distribution, there may be one last stage. Cinema projectors and domestic equipment are not normally capable of showing film in **Sepmag** form. To make prints for general distribution, the magnetic sound may be turned into a combined **Optical Sound Track (Comopt)**.

The advantage of an optical sound track is that, because it is a photographic recording of the sound, it can be printed with the picture in one process and the resulting 'married print' contains both picture and sound. The disadvantage is that optical tracks are of relatively poor quality when compared to magnetically recorded sound.

The system is only really useful where a large number of identical prints have to be made and distributed and is rarely used by television except for overseas sales.

The processes described above are common to every type of film production. There are, however, some embellishments which the Director may require and which may need additional processes.

Film Editing

ROSTRUM CAMERA

This is a system for filming and giving apparent movement to still photographs and artwork. In its simplest form, a camera is bolted vertically over a table on which the artwork can be manipulated in any direction as it is photographed frame by frame or continuously for zooms, pans and other movements. Animated cartoons are the most complicated products of **rostrum camera work** and these days require sophisticated computerised techniques. What must be remembered is that rostrum camera work is a time-consuming process and the facilities are not always readily available, so a Director should allow himself several weeks leeway for booking camera time.

The rostrum area

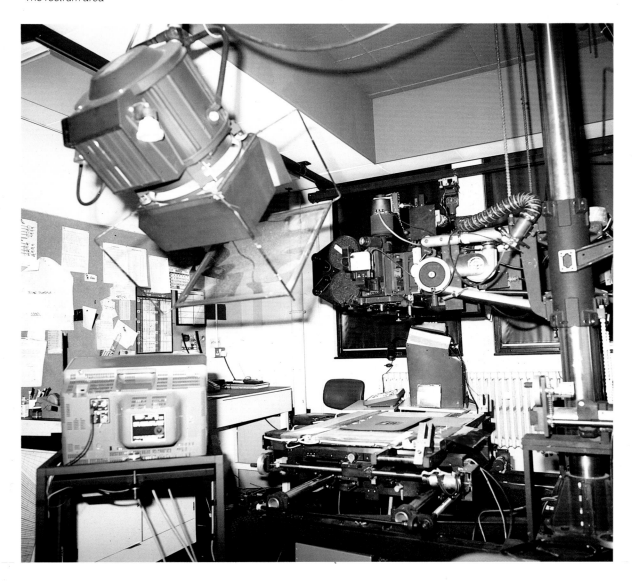

GRAPHICS

Artwork is produced by a Graphic Artist. This may be a number of simple name captions or complex animation sequences. In the case of animated cartoons, the Graphics Artist may also supervise the shooting of the film. Lettering is normally filmed on a clear background for subsequent combination with the programme pictures. When the artwork has been completed and put on to film, the resulting negative and print are sent to the Film Editor for inclusion in the body of the programme.

ARCHIVE FILM

There are many specialized film libraries which hold collections of historic film material. The rights to this material are often expensive and the process of searching for it and arranging to view it can be very time consuming. Don't commit yourself to using archive material until you know exactly how much it is going to cost you and without knowing that you have plenty of time for your picture research. Often, the material will only exist on 35mm film in which case a 16mm reduction print will have to be made. Very old original film material can also be on a nitrate base which becomes very dangerous and unstable with age and may need special arrangements for copying.

OPTICALS

Opticals are special effects produced by the film laboratories, the most common of which are **freeze frames**, **fades** and **step printing** which gives the impression of speeding up or slowing down film. There are some extremely complicated optical effects available but, whatever the problem, the process is the same. The Film Editor gives precise instructions to the laboratory using the key numbers as a reference. The original negative is sent to the optical printer which, for the purpose of explanation, can be regarded as a projector pointing at a camera. There is a space in the middle to put various masks for wipes, binocular effects, keyhole irises, etc. The original negative is laced into the 'projection' side of the optical printer and the unexposed film, which will become the **optical negative**, is laced into the camera side. When the opticals have been made, effectively re-photographing the original negatives with the various effects required, the new optical negative is printed, and then optical negative and print are returned to the cutting room for inclusion in the main cutting copy of the film.

Although film remains more than a match for video in almost all aspects of shooting and editing, it is in the realm of optical effects that videotape has a clear advantage. Digital effects generators of ever-increasing sophistication enable the Director to manipulate pictures in infinite permutations. For this reason many television film makers transfer their graded prints to videotape for optical and graphic work.

Creative Picture Editing

The art of picture editing is proof positive that 'the whole can be greater than the sum of its parts'. In the 1920's, the Russian film-maker Vsevolod Pudovkin demonstrated the subjective power of editing by a very simple experiment. He intercut a close-up of the famous Russian actor Mosjukhin with three other shots. One shot was a plate of food, the second was a child at play, and the third was the corpse of an old woman. Those who saw the sequence remarked on the brilliant subtlety of the actor's facial expressions. His face seemed to register pleasant anticipation at the prospect of an excellent meal, gentle warmth at the child's pleasure, and compassion for the hard life of the old woman who was finally at peace. But, in fact, the actor had been directed to hold a blank expression and had no idea of the intercuts that the Director had in mind. For Pudovkin, separate shots were like separate words which gain their full meaning in the context of the sentence. This process by which the construction of film gives emphasis and meaning to shots, which of themselves may be bland images, is the key to creative film editing and is as important to the documentary maker as to the Director of drama.

If we have a shot of a man walking through a door and a bucket of whitewash falls on his head, it is possible that the audience will laugh. If we have a shot of the man walking along the corridor before he enters the booby-trapped room, there will be no less laughter but, importantly, no more laughter. However, if the sequence starts with a shot of the bucket in position, there should be a far stronger reaction from the audience as they can now anticipate the consequences of entering the room. If there is no shot of the bucket in position, the Editor cannot build up the anticipation. The Director needs to visualise the finished sequence before he starts to shoot it. Only then can he guarantee to provide the Editor with the shots required to deliver the maximum effect.

Time and place

In all single-camera shooting, the realities of time and place undergo a metamorphosis. Shots that may have taken several hours to achieve or have been completed at quite different times can be cut together with apparent spontaneity and continuity of action. In one scene two lovers may part by the Eiffel Tower and the man leave shot. If the Editor then cuts to a shot of him getting into a car and driving off (a shot actually filmed on the studio lot in London), there is no reason why the audience should not believe that he has just walked a few yards to his car and that he has not, in fact, crossed the Channel and been filmed again days later.

However, editing is a self-effacing art so it is the responsibility of the Director to provide shots which readily cut together. A wide shot with two actors, a man left of frame looking right towards a woman right of frame looking left, will easily cut to a close-up of the man or a close-up of a woman, but only if they are still looking in the same direction. This might seem so blindingly obvious that it is a waste of print to mention it, but it is amazing how many times such a simple rule is broken.

Creative Picture Editing

BASIC HINTS

Drama

If the Director obeys a few simple rules, the Editor is likely to have a much easier time cutting the shots together:

- In a scene involving two actors, never plan to cut from one two-shot to another — however different the angle may be. The chances of both actors' continuity being exactly the same at the cut point are zero.

- **Master shots** containing a whole scene, can prove to be both expensive and superfluous. A shot that is wide enough to contain all the action of a long dialogue scene will probably be too wide when cut to half-way through the scene and is generally a waste of time. Certainly start and end a scene with the traditional wide establisher — if that is your style — but, once you have decided the point at which to go in close, the wide shot is redundant and a waste of film to continue to shoot.

  Sometimes a nervous Director feels that if he takes a master he has at least 'got cover' on the scene. This is a fallacy because the extreme width of the master shot usually looks ugly if it is used in the middle of the scene. Of course, wide shots can work brilliantly at any point in a scene if there is a dramatic point for them and they are planned. Film direction is all about planning for the desired effect.

- **Cutting on action** always works well and can often cover for bad continuity. If we have a wide shot of a girl walking towards a park bench and she sits down, a cut to the closer-shot as she sits will look smoother than cutting just before or just after she sits. If — heaven forbid — her handbag has changed hands between shots, there is less likelihood that this will be noticed if the cut is made on the action.

  A scene involving **dialogue** has to be carefully directed for action cuts, so that the moves occur on exactly the same words. It is safer to leave the actual move clear of dialogue. For example:

  GEORGE: My God I'm tired.

  (HE SLUMPS INTO THE ARMCHAIR)

  If the plan is to cut from a wide shot of George to a close-up as he slumps in the chair, then ask the actor to play the dialogue before or just after the sit, but *not* during it.

- When a dialogue scene is cut together, the Editor frequently overlaps the sound of one actor over the close-up of the other. The pace of the performance can be varied considerably in the cutting room; indeed, many screen actors owe at least some of their reputation to the Editor's sense of timing. But the Editor can only cut overlapping dialogue successfully if the close-ups are taken clean, that is, with none of the actors' lines overlapping each other at the time of performance. It is particularly difficult in, for example, a scene

Creative Picture Editing

involving a heated argument, when the artists would naturally be treading on each other's lines. Trust to technique and shoot the two-shot with as many natural overlaps as you like, but when you come to the close-ups, allow a sufficient gap between the lines to 'get the scissors in' (and don't be afraid to ask the Sound Recordist for advice).

- Both actors and Film Editor will thank you if you start each shot a couple of lines earlier than the point at which you actually intend to cut to it. If the shot 'holds' past the point that you plan to cut out, it is sensible to keep turning anyway.

Taking all the above points into consideration, consider the following stage directions and suggested simple plan for filming this scene.

SALLY IS LYING ON THE LIVING-ROOM SOFA READING A BOOK. COLIN ENTERS AND KISSES HER ON THE HEAD — HE KNEELS BY SALLY AND THEY CHAT. SALLY RISES AND GOES TO THE FRENCH DOORS. COLIN FOLLOWS HER AND CONVERSATION ENSUES.

① Wide shot. Colin enters

② 2-Shot Kiss

③ CU Sally

④ CU Colin

⑤ Wide shot developing to 2-Shot as Colin follows Sally

① CU Sally reading

② MS Colin at door developing to ......

③ Colin crossing to Sally for kiss

Creative Picture Editing

The basic shots for such a scene are (see **Storyboard** p.18):

Wide shot showing Sally on the sofa and taking in Colin's entrance. Shortly after the kiss, the Director could cut the camera and go into a close two-shot, planning to make an action cut on the kiss. The scene would then be played in this two-shot up to the point where Sally gets up and moves to the French doors; the Director would then cut just after she has left the frame. The same piece of dialogue would then be covered again on a close-up of Sally and a close-up of Colin — again these close-ups would cut at Sally's move.

The Director would then take a wide shot of the room with the camera by the French doors, so that, as Sally gets up, she walks close to camera and Colin, following her, forms another close two-shot. This shot would start just before Sally's rise and would be from a different angle than the opening wide shot. The scene could then be completed with singles of Sally and Colin if necessary.

It is, however, rather obvious to start the scene on a wide shot. A close-up of Sally reading her book, cutting to the wide shot as she reacts to Colin's entrance, would probably look better. A developing shot, taking Colin from the doorway to the sofa and forming the two-shot for the kiss, would also be slicker, but the basic outline above would work and is included as an example of the minimum an Editor has the right to expect.

The dangers of cutting from wide shot to wide shot are clearly evident below. As well as looking ugly the shift of camera angle appears to have moved the secretary's position. The symmetry of the set adds to the confusion ....

Creative Picture Editing

- When you take close-ups, make sure they exclude distracting appendages — nose, ears, hair, etc. of the other actor.

- **Over the shoulder** two-shots can be useful: in such shots the other actor's hair, ears, etc. can obviously be shown.

- The Sound Editor needs the atmosphere after the final words on each take, so take care not to say CUT too soon — allow about three seconds. Sometimes actors are a little too quick off the mark when you say ACTION; again, it is helpful if there is a beat after ACTION before the dialogue begins.

- Whenever you shoot a **developing shot**, pay particular attention to the performance and the timing, as the Editor will not be able to use a close-up to adjust the internal timing of the scene.

The Director should always be aware that editing is not just a matter of making a smooth cut from one shot to another. It is possible for a film to consist of a series of the most brilliantly smooth edits and still be dreadful. Editing is as much to do with pace and construction as it is with cutting from shot to shot.

Documentary

Shaping and pacing are vital to the success of any documentary. The following — if acted upon — will help your Film Editor.

- Whenever possible, shoot the **interviews** for a documentary first. The items discussed may need illustrative material and you won't know what that is until after the interview.

- When you are filming someone at work — making a cupboard, fixing a car, working at a bench, etc. — shoot close-ups of the face concentrating on the work, tools being picked out of the tool box — any useful shots that will allow you to condense the time the process takes.

- Always have an idea of how long the screen time of each item is likely to be. If an individual is incidental to the main thrust of the documentary, he or she is unlikely to occupy more than one-and-a-half minutes of screen time, so adjust your shooting ratio accordingly.

- Ask the Cameraman to hold the front and end of any zooms or pans so they can be used as individual shots. Zooms and pans are nearly always too long when they are seen in the cold light of the cutting room. If there is time, try them at a couple of different speeds. If in doubt repeat the action in two directions; e.g. hold a shot, zoom in, hold the end of the first shot for several seconds, then zoom out again to the beginning and hold.

- If you are shooting a sequence which is likely to involve **picture mixes**, don't say CUT too soon. See the action to its natural close and count five, then you can cut.

Creative Picture Editing

- If an Interviewee is boring, no amount of cutaways or editing tricks will alter the fact.

- Never forget the power of **sound** to draw attention to visual detail. In a crowd shot, a mother holding a baby may well go unnoticed, but dub a baby crying on to the sound track and all eyes will go to the mother.

- The Editor's greatest service to you ought to be objectivity. You might have overcome all manner of difficulties in order to get a magnificent shot and understandably be loath to lose it. But if it has no place in the film, the Editor should tell you. The same applies to the sequences with which you are in love but which are, in fact, redundant. A good Editor can be your greatest protection against self-indulgence (cf. 'You must learn to murder your children'. *W.H. Auden*).

- One of the most cost effective editing procedures can take place at the scripting stage. A **typed script** for a 30-minute play will run to about 60 pages. If it has 85 pages it needs cutting before you shoot a frame!

Just as shots will not cut together effectively unless directed accordingly, so sequences will not build up to a climax unless their direction has been pre-planned. Take the classic example of a Western gun fight (see **Storyboard** p.22). As the bad guy and the hero walk towards each other down the main street, two factors will build a sense of tension. Firstly, the inter-cut shots of hero and bad guy will become shorter and shorter (editing) and, secondly, the shots will become tighter and tighter (direction) up to the point where the two gunslingers draw and one of them drops dead. A haphazardly shot sequence could still avail itself of the editing devices, but would be less successful because of the lack of direction (and visual build). Again, it is inescapable that the construction of a sequence *requires planning from the outset*.

Avoiding problems

It may be a cliché, but a film needs a beginning, a middle and an end. If the Director concerns himself with the construction of the film from the outset, there will be fewer problems in the cutting room. Nothing is more time consuming than the attempt to edit mountains of ill-considered footage into some intelligent and intelligible form. This is particularly true in the documentary field.

A documentary film can be nursed into powerful life if the Director constantly asks himself a few key questions and provides detailed and 'thought-through' answers to them.

- What is the film about?

- Who needs to appear and how is their contribution to be reflected?

- What stance is the film going to take (for/against, questioning, or purely informative)?

Specimen Storyboard: Gun Fight

Six-plate Steenbeck

- Are any side issues illuminating or merely distracting?
- What is the visual core of the film to be?
- Will music be used, and if so, how and why?

Honest answers to these questions can vitalise the planning and editing of any film.

Documentary films for television today reflect a curious mixture of styles. In the mid-1950's, Dennis Mitchell made a number of excellent films reflecting everyday life in English and American towns. These films had their style based on the solid foundations laid by Grierson in the 1930's, but Mitchell invented one very telling and infinitely useful device, the **voice-over**. Combined with the commentary, and sometimes replacing commentary altogether, Mitchell used the voices of people who appeared in the films.

The 1960's saw the birth of the *Tonight* programme. A number of talented journalists from the recently defunct *Picture Post* were brought together to make a wide variety of short films for inclusion in the *Tonight* programme's magazine format. Their films were short and often very entertaining, but what has come to pass for technique at that time was more to do with the logistics of getting stories on the air than any considered development of 'documentary' as an art form. Most of the films were simple and had the strong anchor of the reporter's personality to save them. Editing and cinematography were often rudimentary and sometimes even crude.

There is a danger that inexperienced Documentary Directors may adopt a rag-bag of editing devices from the past without a full understanding of the ingredients that held the films of a previous decade together. Voice-overs become tedious and self-conscious if the pictures used to accompany them have scant relevance to the words. Many television documentaries of the late 1960's and early 1970's were riddled with this fault, the pictures degenerating to 'wallpaper' and leaving ideas to be communicated by the sound track alone.

A potent ingredient of the film sound track is music. Music in Documentary will most usually be taken from mood disc or copyright-clearable commercial discs. This has the advantage that the music is available to the Director and Editor at the start of the editing process. The music will therefore take its natural place on the weft and warp of the film. If you can afford the luxury of specially-composed music, then do remember to leave room in the construction of your film for the music to have space to breathe. The danger with specially composed is that the film seems limp without music and therefore is cut 'too tight', too tight for a successful inclusion of the music at the later stage.

If there is one hard and fast rule for the film-maker, it is that picture and sound together set the scene, tell the story and convey the atmosphere. Sound may sometimes be subservient to picture, but picture must *never* be subservient to sound. Editing should always obey this most golden of rules.

Editing Videotape

Editing videotape involves the same artistic and editorial decisions as does editing film. The design and picture characteristics of video equipment are being modified all the time to make them increasingly similar to film. The working methods of crews are also almost identical, whether they are working in film or video. As the two technologies converge, the difference between working in one or the other is being reduced to little more than the difference in shooting film on two different types of film stock. The main remaining difference is that most current video shooting involves sound and picture being recorded on the same tape. But it is now possible to link a video camera to an independent quarter-inch tape recorder or to a half-inch video recorder used for sound only. At the time of writing, technological change is taking place at such speed that, while no single solution to the sound with picture problem has yet prevailed, it can be predicted that video techniques will increasingly converge with the proven successful techniques of film. It is in the post production stages that the real differences between the two media become apparent.

FORMATS

Originally broadcast quality videotape was restricted to the very cumbersome two-inch reel-to-reel 'quad' tapes. This was thoroughly unsuitable for location work and early editing actually involved physically cutting and joining tapes. As sound and picture existed on the same tape in parallel, the resulting editing process was not particularly fast or sophisticated even when the cutting of the videotape was replaced by a 'dubbing' technique. Recently, however, there has been an explosion to alternative formats. These are briefly:

One-inch reel-to-reel tape

This gives very high quality images capable of going through several 'generations' without excessive loss of quality. Portable one-inch recorders for location work are available, but generally this format is preferred for studio and outside broadcast recording purposes. Many broadcast organisations shoot on location with a smaller and more flexible format but then 'dump' the rushes on to one-inch copies before beginning to edit. One-inch is the favourite format for transmitting programmes and film transmission prints are often transferred to it for convenience of presentation.

Three-quarter-inch video cassette

The system using three-quarter-inch tape is called **U-Matic**. For location recording purposes, the cassettes are of 20-minutes duration and fit into a portable recorder similar to a Nagra quarter-inch tape recorder. With most current systems, this has to be connected by cable to the camera thus restricting the flexibility of the operation. Systems of radio links have been devised however. In the U.S.A., Japan and countries using the NTSC 525-line television system, there is only a single kind of U-Matic. But with the European PAL or SECAM 625 system U-Matic comes in two types which are known as High Band and Low Band. **High Band** picture quality approaches one-inch in the first generation and is recognised as achieving broadcast quality. It can be edited to about three generations without too much degradation of the picture. A drawback of this system is that the recording equipment is comparatively expensive. **Low band** is very similar and considerably cheaper and is the favourite format for industrial and closed circuit purposes. However, loss of quality is marked if the editing involves going through more than two generations. This may be partly solved by 'dumping' the rushes on to High Band or one-inch at the beginning of post production. Many countries now accept Low Band for broadcast purposes simply for reasons of economy. In terms of shooting, it may be regarded as identical to the more up-market High Band.

Half-inch format

Two professional systems using half-inch format now exist. These are the **VHS M(II)-format** and the **Betacam (SP)** system. There is no compatibility with their domestic equivalents (VHS and Betamax) except in the design of the cassettes they use. Betacam seems to be the current favourite in Europe. The cassettes are of approximately 24-minutes duration and fit into the body of the camera in the same way as a loaded magazine into a film camera. Sound may be recorded directly on the tape by either a microphone cable or radio link. These are the first professional videotape formats to offer a flexibility that approaches film. The cameras are similar in weight and operate much the same as a modern film camera. The picture quality of these is reputedly as good as that of one-inch: however, the cost of the MII or the record/playback machines needed to set up an all-Beta editing suite is high and many organisations which shoot on them still prefer to transfer the rushes to another format for post production.

Advances in video head and tape design have allowed the production of a video cassette format using 8mm wide tape and have led to the upgrading of the domestic VHS format to Super VHS (S-VHS). This system provides pictures which are of a quality suitable for use by non-broadcast corporate video producers. Standard VHS tapes can be played on a S-VHS machine, but not vice versa.

Digital VTRS

Digital videotape recorders provide an almost transparent medium for recording, replaying and editing video pictures and sound. The signal is converted into a series of digits (binary numbers) which are then recorded on to the tape. Picture degradation does not occur when multiple generation copies are made. The cost of these machines, however, precludes their use in all but the most sophisticated environment.

The future

Such has been the pace of change, it is predictable that tape itself is obsolescent and that **solid state** recording systems may be with us before long. The final judgement on any of these breakthroughs will not be made on the basis of their engineering cleverness alone. Cost will be a factor, but the main obstacles to their acceptance outside the amateur market will be the ease or difficulty of the post production operation.

Editing Videotape

Videotape edit suite

In some respects, videotape editing remains behind the mechanically simple, yet effective, medium of film. Both film and video have their respective advantages at the post production stage, but until all the post production problems are solved, it will be irrelevant to anyone other than an engineer whether a programme is recorded on reel-to-reel, cassette, a bubble memory or a length of wet string.

VIDEOTAPE POST PRODUCTION

In film, the sound track is separate from the film stock from the very beginning of shooting, and both sound and picture can be physically *broken down* into different shots once the editor starts work. As a result, it is possible to move, shorten or lengthen shots at any stage of the editing process and reverse the order of sequences without having to change anything else in the programme. It is, therefore, the flexibility of editing which explains the popularity of film against video with many Directors. Even at the last moment, detailed changes can be made with the minimum of difficulty.

Some productions on videotape, to achieve greater flexibility, try to combine the two technologies by transferring all sound tracks to 16mm magnetic film, cutting the video pictures first, and then laying sound tracks with a film pic sync to be subsequently dubbed as with film. There is even the possibility of transferring the rough assembled video rushes on to a film print and then continuing totally in the film medium up to the negative cutting stage when the video pictures are edited from the master tapes and combined with the dubbed final film sound mix.

However, the remarks which follow are concerned with videotape editing pure and simple. Because it is not practicable physically to cut the tape and all videotape editing these days is done by copying the original pictures in the required order on to second tape, known as the second generation. In other words, the programme has to be built up step-by-step from the beginning and in sequence. This s known as **dub editing**.

Most video recorders have simple electronic editing devices built into them and at the press of a button a programme can be built up with clean cuts in vision and with some sound manipulation; e.g. stopping and starting incoming and outgoing sound at different points from the picture cuts. This is simple editing and is the relatively crude method used, for example, in the fast cutting of News programmes. To do this the fullest possible details of the intended assembly with accurate timings are needed, because any subsequent changes will mean going back to the beginning. This means either a complete re-edit or going to a third or more generations. With every successive generation, there is a degradation of the picture quality which in the case of Low Band U-Matic operation, can be disastrous. So it follows that video pictures should go through as few generations as possible. However, this problem can now be avoided if the recording can be made using digital machines.

Editing Videotape

If digital machines are not available, many Directors resolve the situation by using what is called **off-line** editing. In its simplest form, this means taking the original rushes and watching them repeatedly to mark down the timings and preparing a comprehensive assembly order before even entering the edit suite. In some cases, it is possible to 'dump' the rushes on to a cheaper domestic format like half-inch VHS or Betamax cassettes and then physically construct an assembly to give the Video Editor a near-finished product to copy. It is a matter of debate as to how much time and effort is actually saved this way in a television production.

But even here the choices for further major revision are limited. Picture and sound still have to be built up in sequence from beginning to end and it is not possible, as in film, easily to remove an objectionable passage or add extra footage. Decisions about cutting points, music and sound effects, have to be made one at a time and are difficult to change later. This limitation has, to an extent, held back the adoption of videotape for many television programmes apart from in News and Current Affairs where immediacy and economy are more important than the absolute technical quality of the product or in multi-camera studio work where editing decisions are to a great extent taken in advance. But computer manufacturers have come to the aid of the producers and videotape editing is finally coming of age.

Editing in VT

The key to the process is known as **time code**. Basically, this means that during recording, every frame of the tape is marked with a number representing the time of day, the time since the beginning of the shoot or elapsed tape duration in hours, minutes, seconds and frames. All this signifies is that every frame may be uniquely identified in the same way as rubber numbering on film. Although invisible on normal playback, the time code can be summoned up as a visual display on the picture by the equipment in the editing suite. Location **shot lists** are kept according to slate numbers the same as film, but also to the time code which can be read off a counter on the camera or recorder. As a result, production staff can log and appraise each picture frame by frame.

Time code

By using this electronic reference, the editing equipment can commit all information to a computer memory. The result is that the Director and Videotape or Picture Editor can hereafter play around with the pictures as much as they like and retain each final decision in the computer's memory. Only when they want a final print need they tell the computer to go back to square one and print a final transmission copy. This may include visual effects such as mixes, fades, etc., as well as complex sound mixes. The end result is that the final programme is still only a second generation copy however many times the rushes have been modified.

So, effectively, the whole editing and re-editing process has taken place **off-line** because the final print is electronically assembled from the original rush tapes and is only one generation removed from the original. This is the **on line** copy.

Editing Videotape

THE VIDEO EDIT SUITE

For anything more sophisticated than the most simple 'knife and fork' editing, three machines are needed, two to replay tapes and one to serve as a record machine. The output of the two playback machines is routed through a vision mixing desk to the record machine. Some form of computer control is needed to ensure that each play machine can cue up at the proper place to enable the vision mixing desk to achieve mixes, wipes, etc. on demand.

Sound tracks

All videotapes carry at least two high-quality sound tracks which can be edited along with the picture. This may be quite adequate for a great deal of location work like interviews, but clearly falls short of laying and mixing the six or more different tracks which is commonplace at a film dub. To compensate for this, the video edit suite can be equipped with a multi-track audio tape recorder, a disc player or any number of quarter-inch tape recorders. In this way, complex sound effects can be built up just as with film and are all electronically linked to the picture by the ubiquitous time code. Of course, an essential piece of additional equipment to make this possible is a sound mixing desk.

Picture editing, therefore, remains a comparatively simple operation, but the editing of the sound tracks remains the most difficult problem.

How can we achieve a basic mixed sound track using two audio tracks on the original videotape, a six-channel sound mixing desk and an ordinary quarter-inch tape recorder?

To start with, most simple edit suites are designed to operate in either an **assemble mode** or an **insert mode**. Assemble mode involves the simple stitching together of sounds and pictures in sequence on to a totally blank tape. It is best to avoid this mode of editing, as it can be very limiting, and is often impossible for sound and vision to be edited separately.

Insert mode

To operate in the **insert mode**, the tape on the record machine must previously have been recorded with what is known as **colour black**. This is **continuous black level and colour burst**. This colour black signal provides the VTR with a set of reference pulses for video and colour. This reference can be thought of as 'electronic, sprocket holes'.

Once this has been done it is possible to begin editing both sound tracks separately from each other and from the picture track. Sophisticated manipulation of sound and picture also becomes possible, in a way that cannot be achieved in **assemble mode** which necessitates the cutting of sound and picture together.

So if a programme has been shot on standard lightweight video equipment in anticipation of a final product which will combine music, effects, location sound and recorded commentary, how do the Director and Editor construct the sound part of the final programme, given that the editing of the pictures by themselves presents no special problems?

Assembly

After viewing all the material and noting the usable takes, an **assembly order** is made up by the Director. Then, using a tape previously recorded with black level and colour burst, the Editor begins to construct the programme. Working from the assembly order, he may produce an **editing running order** as follows:

Video	Sound
Opening titles	Music
Presenter piece to camera	Sync location
Cutaways	Location sound
Sequence shot for music	*Music with location effects
Interview	Mix music into interview
Cutaways to cover interview	Interview sound only
	Mix effects (FX) into music
Sequence for music	*Music with location effects
Closing piece to camera	Lose music in location sound
Closing titles	With music

*Commentary to be written for these music sequences.

The process which follows closely approximates to A&B roll cutting or chequerboarding in film.

As the first part of the programme consists of pictures cut to music, the music is laid on to Audio Track 1 of the record machine before any pictures are edited. This enables the Editor to 'cut' the pictures accurately to the musical phrasing. At the end of this first musical item a Presenter on location introduces the subject of the programme. It is necessary to ensure that the location sound is edited on to Audio Track 2 of the record machine.

To give a smooth transition between music and location sound when laying the audio on to the record tape, ensure that an overlap between the music and the location sound occurs i.e.

Audio Track 1   ....Music

Audio Track 2   Location Sound ....

This overlap enables a mix to be performed at a later time.

Following the Presenter piece, which has its sound laid on to Audio Track 2 of the record machine, the Director requires another music sequence. This music is again laid on to Audio Track 1 before any pictures are edited, overlapping the location sound, enabling a mix to be performed later, i.e.

Audio Track 1   Music ....

Audio Track 2 ....Location Sound

However, at this point the Director requires sync effects to be mixed with the music, so these effects are edited along with

Editing Videotape

their relevant pictures on to Audio Track 2, ensuring smooth joins between the edited effects, and also ensuring that the sound for the Presenter piece is left complete.

The net result of this process, finally, is that two sound tracks are constructed. Track 1 containing all relevant music and Track 2 containing the edited Presenter pieces which were originally recorded on location, along with desired sound effects, also recorded on location or taken (if no relevant sound effects were available at the location) from quarter-inch tape and edited into the correct sequence on to Audio Track 2.

This can be diagrammatically represented as follows. Compare with the original editing log.

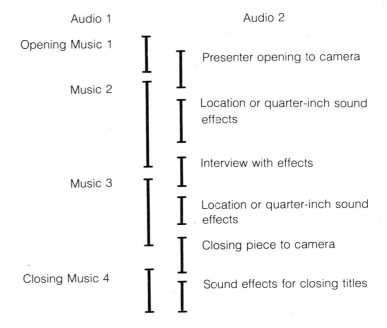

Audio 1	Audio 2
Opening Music 1	Presenter opening to camera
Music 2	Location or quarter-inch sound effects
	Interview with effects
Music 3	Location or quarter-inch sound effects
	Closing piece to camera
Closing Music 4	Sound effects for closing titles

Editing Videotape

The sound is said to be **chequerboarded** when arranged in this manner on to the videotape.

The next process consists of laying the edited pictures along with a mix of this sound on to another tape. Therefore, the edited tape is taken out of the record machine and put into the replay machine. A new tape is placed in the record machine.

The Video Editor then mixes, at the appropriate times, the two previously assembled sound tracks on to Audio Track 1 of the new record tape. It is most important that the picture is copied alongside the sound, as this gives a synchronising reference when laying the completed sound track back on to the original pictures.

At this point the **commentary** is written with reference to the associated pictures. When the Director is satisfied with the script, the commentary is recorded against the pictures on to Audio Track 2 of the second tape, resulting in:

Audio 1	Audio 2	
		Commentary
Presenter sound, music and effects mixed together		
		Commentary

N.B. Again compare with the original editing order.

There are, at this point, two videotapes, *one* containing edited pictures and two sound tracks:

Audio 1 — Music
Audio 2 — Effects and location sound.

The *second* contains a copy of the edited pictures and two sound tracks:

Audio 1 — A mix of music and location sound
Audio 2 — Commentary.

The two Audio Tracks of the *second* tape are then mixed together at appropriate times and laid back on to Audio Track 2 of the *original* edited picture tape. The original edited picture tape *must* be used because video pictures are degraded by copying.

The final sound track on Audio Track 2 is now complete and has all the required components of music, location sound and commentary mixed together by the Video Editor under the control of the programme Director, in the relative quiet of the self-contained edit suite.

Editing Videotape

REC/EDIT VTR   TAPE 1

Video   Audio 1   Audio 2

Original Edited Pictures

Music

Music

Music

Music

Mix of Music, Location Sound, Effects and Commentary making up the MASTER Sound Track

N.B. ONLY Audio Track 2 is used for transmission.

Shooting on location

This process of sound mixing is equally applicable to all tape formats. It should be noted, however, that one-inch video recorders have at least three, and possibly four, audio tracks. Track 3 is normally used to carry the time code information. To reiterate, sound editing and mixing should be carried out in the **insert mode**.

The use of time code and computers allows the programme maker the freedom to construct sophisticated sound tracks, and to try out any optical effects at the time of editing without having to wait for a dub, or the labs to return processed 'film opticals'. Changes of mind are thereby easily and quickly achieved.